DIGITAL MONSOON

Siddhartha Bose is a poet, playwright and performer based in London. His poetry has appeared in *Voice Recognition: 21 Poets for the 21st Century* (Bloodaxe, 2009), *Dear World and Everyone in It: New Poetry in the UK* (Bloodaxe, 2013) and *The HarperCollins Book of English Poetry* (HarperCollins, 2012). His first book, *Kalagora*, appeared in 2010 from Penned in the Margins. Siddhartha has been featured on BBC Four, BBC Radio 3 and was dubbed one of the 'ten rising stars of British poetry' by *The Times*.

Siddhartha wrote and performed *Kalagora*, which completed an acclaimed run at Edinburgh Festival Fringe 2011. His second show, *London's Perverted Children*, was longlisted for an Oxford Samuel Becket Theatre Trust Award. He is a Leverhulme Fellow in Drama at Queen Mary, University of London.

ALSO BY SIDDHARTHA BOSE

Kalagora (Penned in the Margins, 2010)

Digital Monsoon

Siddhartha Bose

Penned in the Margins
LONDON

PUBLISHED BY PENNED IN THE MARGINS
Toynbee Studios, 28 Commercial Street, London E1 6AB
www.pennedinthemargins.co.uk

All rights reserved
© Siddhartha Bose 2013

The right of Siddhartha Bose to be identified as the author of this work has been asserted by him in accordance with Section 77 of the Copyright, Designs and Patent Act 1988.

This book is in copyright. Subject to statutory exception and to provisions of relevant collective licensing agreements, no reproduction of any part may take place without the written permission of Penned in the Margins.

First published 2013

Printed in the United Kingdom by Bell & Bain Ltd.

ISBN
978-1-908058-16-4

This book is sold subject to the condition that it shall not, by way of trade or otherwise, be lent, re-sold, hired out, or otherwise circulated without the publisher's prior consent in any form of binding or cover other than that in which it is published and without a similar condition including this condition being imposed on the subsequent purchaser.

Contents

Kapoor's Temenos	13
LDN	15
Wicklove	18
What the Bass Said	22
Holography	25
Indigo, Bandra	31
Doctor Sahib	33
Proverbs	35
Cybosaurus	39
Mediterranean	55
The Muckworm	57
The Living and the Dead	59
Once Upon a Time in New York	62
Digital Monsoon	65
Hackney Fragments	67
Ricorso	71

Acknowledgements

The author would like to thank the editors of the following journals and anthologies in which some poems from this book first appeared: *Dear World and Everyone in It: New Poetry in the UK*, *Lung Jazz: Young British Poets for Oxfam*, *The Wolf*, *The Eye of Temenos*, *Tears in the Fence*, *Likestarlings* and *Acquired for Development By: A Hackney Anthology*. Poems in this book also appeared in *London's Perverted Children*, which premiered in London in 2012. An early version of 'The Living and The Dead' was written for *Komagata Maru* (WhyNotTheatre, Toronto); the title is inspired by a short story by Rabindranath Tagore. 'Kapoor's Temenos' is dedicated to Andy Willoughby and Bob Beagrie.

Special thanks to Tom Chivers, *il miglior fabbro*, for his invaluable guidance in editing, shaping and structuring this book.

Thanks always to my mother, Sushmita Bose, and to Maria. This book is for my grandfather, who was once a Londoner.

D.K. Bose (1911-83)

Digital Monsoon

You have to belong to a place
before you are qualified to speak
Iain Sinclair

Kapoor's Temenos

I

Dog-whoof, spin-wharf,
>   gluttoned like a matrix. Curves of barbed wire.
>   Sky-shape tarot card.

>   Ear-cunt on arches.

Interstellar elongation, you surprise like a
>   spider, crawling out of that
>   goon-fog of a Middlesborough morning.

>   Stretched like a sleeping dinosaur. Temenos.

The air hints of smack, glass-crack, guillotined head-chops. My friends like medieval scops
>   turntable tales of rise, decay, fall.
>   Tumble-town, this once was a steel-centre (Tenter-

hook me, heathen across oceans). Now, shut-factory tunes gloam like ghosts (I see Hamlet's teeth edging from shroud of water). Productive darkness.

Ravens appear, crib-caged, like babies. Pubs rake like skinheads. College hipsters artfully pour their graces. And there, above all, watching

Temenos — dog-space divinity.
(No more steel or ships. Or slaves.)

II

And you, mangled creator of space-art — mimic-man-cosma.
You left Bombay years ago (city of chatter-gods,
    mammon-fested monster.)

You journeyed from gray oceans, shifted imperially here,
    fashioned an accent out of breathing blood-clots. Peeled
    brown-skin from ivory-bone
    with ancient knives, to pupa yourself to a demi-god,
    poshed and polished.

Archetypal autocrat, scanning the fog of northern England, you create mirrors o' yourself.

And there you are Anish bhai, locked with your visions on a foggy Middlesborough morning —

    tentacled,

            cockroached,

                  infinite.

LDN

I

A small black-box room in Hackney Wick. Outside are beatboxers, laughing, tickling each other in sound-feathers. Spitting oracles, airpockets, patterned webs. Inside, an émigré writer wretches, tears pages of books, sticks them together piecemeal. Kills spiders for inspiration. A girl he brought home once felt instant fear, saying that in the mountains of Carthage a man living in a room within four walls is the loneliest creature on earth. He remembers and laughs with smoke in his chest.

II

The city outside is ghostly. It's night-lit, and he sees the streets through the calcified scenes in a little book he's read predicting apocalypse in London. Memories of uprisings against police control beamed over the known universe. Financial meltdown, racial strife, the homeless begging for change outside tube stations.

It snowed last week, and the ice in the streets is bone marrow. Cartilage alleys with garbage bins and the colour of council estate clotheslines. In winter nights this amputated limb of the city is full of green shadows. Piles of carcassing car-doors in empty garages, spray-can skulls washing away in corporate rain. Isolated tin can fires, menacing as sentinels in 2001. Bricks on the paper-strewn streets reflect ghosts of the last battle. Concrete island, bludgeoned by highways. Concrete island, surrounded by the hum and scale of the city. Concrete island, revealing its stories as a peeled onion.

III

When the sun's out, the writer emerges from hibernation, runs downstairs to a cafe where they serve him chocolate brownies, warm coffee, empathy. And he has friends there. There's a Russian émigré called Anastasia who bakes bread and blueberry muffins, who's growing older by the day. There's a photographer called Milo, who waxes his moustache, slicks his bald pate with cream shoeshine. Milo insists on calling him 'boy'.

Anastasia would snicker each time she heard this. She'd see the boy immaculate, tearing tissue-strips, licking tissue-paper edges with neat saliva, gumming them together under a hail of cappuccinos, spreading these scroll-sheets on a single wooden table. She'd see him, daily, make a ritual out of eating sugar cubes like horses in a film she'd seen set in her beloved Russia, where blonde-haired nymphs emerged from medieval waters, and male voices groaned in churches. She remembered those horses, their manes and athletic necks straining in slow-motion, foaming the ire of the universe. We don't have a sense of humour she'd mutter to her apron. Behind her, glasses would break and then reassemble.

IV

This late-afternoon, during her five-minute smoke-break, Anastasia approaches, sits beside the scribbler. She watches him intently like she would a caged animal. She takes out a book, hands it over. 'For you, it's by a friend and he tells stories about London — all this...' she says, her arms reaching out to the Lea river, the red of the Orbit circling the Olympic Stadium, her arms stretching, making maps down the canal to Mile End all the way round to Hackney.

Anastasia gets up, goes back to work. The book is covered in collage, black and white images, scanned graffiti. The book is a prehistoric water-cave.

Wicklove

Two years ago I met this cinnamon girl with glasses and a mean-child tribal-smile at the Hackney Wicked festival.

(Her hair fit for the shape of
         brown deserts. When it
                  falls it flecks
the laughter of her gods. Her nose is a cat, leopard lips. Her neck the perfection of a lemon whose green
    bleeds my eyes)

Chicken-shopped, corner-kebabed, glimmer dereliction, Hackney Wick — chromatic — fizzes, bobs, pops in soap bubbles, like commuters on a plunkt escalator.

(How do you make this
        city a spirit, she asks, when
            all you see is a plant without roots?

            She is more than here. My fear is incense.)

~

Outside the fiesta hums — carnival eyes ears hands hips lips edge & slither around the wasteland of white caravans blaring Nirvana, bulldog-chained, locked. Clouds curve & streak like elegant-ringed fingers. Paintbrush pink. Blotched impressions. Carnival raves glow in dungeons under the rush & cum of the highway by Victoria Park sanitation.

On Felstead Street the old Bedlam performers fizzle — old man looking like an Amish prophet, long-haired and black-hatted, limp-walking, stink-pissing. Next to him there's Jude with her whistle-gun laugh, her fractured teeth & glasses. Hovering birdlike over them there's Bigfoot, waddling like a duck, blind & bearded, headed for his four-cheeseburger fix.

    (I wonder what they make of this performed bohemia?)

~

Round them, Hackney erupts. Art imaginings. Studios as prehistoric caves, Fela-music laces the canal, punkstep grinds hard in the Lord Napier, hoodies hunt & sell tornado ketamine, and graffiti — dinosaur bloodstains, magic map-ruins — lead our way.

(Inside we sit surrounded by plants.
        A cat curled, framed window, salmon sky.
                A crane sticks out like a fishbone.

She tells me stories of her ancestral village in Greece, of a lake called Carla full of reincarnated fish. When I say all art is shamanic, she nods, sticking her tongue in my rib-hole.

        Interstellar contortions, mystical fibula.

When I ask about Olympus —
        rivering down a blank alleyway by Fish Island — she,
hair electric, smiles in salt rain.)

~

The first night, in the abandoned car-park with the litter graffiti off White Post Lane — cockroach eyes, space warriors, dragon souls — we pop. She reaches out, ruffles my razor-head, cleaning my aura.

(It's heavy, she says
        in a wink)

She don't like reggae. I cringe.

(Wandering, I
        see the lines on my
           face in a glowing crystal ball in a Spanish squat in
        St. Mary's Church.

        I am more than one person, one place.)

~

At home, we dance to MJ, greet the morning twirling to silk jazz.

(that killer rendition of 'Autumn Leaves' on
        Somethin' Else. The smoke-oil musk in my skin
        kills her. We sleep alone.)

~

Next day I take the stage with beatboxers, throbbing my rhymes. A devil-dread worshipper, shamanic, muscles through the crowd, sinks in mud, trance-hipped and wild, gives me the finger.

Night-time, the wickerman burns, fireflies abound — tribal sound emancipation.

We stray, salting our way to the Peanut Factory. Find ourselves in a net with bouncing balls. We throw them at each other, laughing.

By the canal, we levitate. Fairy monsters. Police helicopters float & cut currents above us. We swat them away, becoming one in defiance.

Below there's Hackney in pink — river-shroud, rave-rotted incantation. Prayers join us in love.

(Morning spills like milk. The sky is molten lead, like a surgeried heart. My child is me.)

What the Bass Said

Switch-hit cyberoptic cave-bass brain-scan
flat-line star-shine fuzzwobble
brutal break stubble
shifting stones wrecking bones
fibering cosmos-threads
orgasmatonic textures
lick the smoke of your tube-trumpet
skaz it with some crack-flutes
hour-glass heroin shoes
switchblade swiss-knife white-light
prize the feds klue them crept-
o'maniac cleptomania blues
shine those hypnotastic grooves
sub-slamming the streets o' Londinium breakin'
them plasma-screen shopwindows them
council house towers then
spraying with our cans our
funosophy makes us those engine-earz of
those bass holocausts
sitar-strummin' dreadlocked matrix gurus
prizefightin' like tenement tantrics
tabla-cummin' beat-choppin'
musical mainlines vein-slick nose-drip
alien-manna from Andromeda
spin those stories o' hipmaster blow
them hipster brains out show

them eat swallow those
float-forces cage-whore fed-fuelled
glitter arcade shopping mall anaesthetica
can you find me a way to reach you?
Cybosaurus-soul *do you wanna be a gangster?*
No this music makes us droid-prophets
purveyors of subatomic post-cool piracy
the hip of the split-skull wobble
the sly-grip of the hook the
grand space-canyon of the drop
fog us no slim-shady cheers
Mos Def it will the Benga-soul
skream-cry them sub-bass slams
soz-blots we are the lost
boyz & dark girls
rate met bet ket krystal
meth musical freedom fighters yes we are
dinosaur-cyborgs bass-slappin' your
soul with shifty space-licks explode
the drum-mecca kabba
the jungle the jungle on
the river sleepin' in galactic snores
space-grid lights
manic monster masses LDN
dark unreal city
no fog no more mister wasteland
dutta dayadhvam damnation
but eerie glottal sounds o'
the streets o'

regal Londinium
bongo-man don't drop me man
keep us flowin' growin' with
skuzzy tunes yes
this be the new bee-bop hip-hop
punk-doo-op o'
shake the strum o' my glandular
excavation we take we shake
the streets the nights like
prison firestarters
fo sho

Holography

London makes you feel differently. I've picked up a habit
for chicken wings and ecstasy. And coke. My nose is bleeding.
I haven't slept for three days, three nights, and now
I'm spending my last ten quid on a cab-ride. And what's more?

I see green all round me. Honest. Everything's green.

The fried chicken shops are green. Sunlight is green.
The council flats bleed green. Pavements are green.
People are green — Bangladeshi, Turkish, African,
ghetto European — all green.

Oyster-advertising cornershops are green. Deadpeople
white bicycle newspaper flowerfilled obituaries
on every streetcorner are green. Hoodies and crackheads

are green. Glint guns are green. Mullah beards and
east London mosques and Brick Lane Jamma-Masjid's
green. Sweaty kebabshops are green. Afterhours
whitelight diners are green. Yuppies and bobos in Broadway Market
sipping their leper-chocolaty cappuccinos are green.
Their faux French la-vie-en-rose restobars are green.

The toothless dopeheads with dogs and newspaper smacksellers
with caved-in cheeks on the edge of London Fields are green.
Hackney Central new condos and couples prampushing their tots

are green.

Chinese DVD sellers at the junkyard carpark by Bohemia cafe by the tantric Tesco by the overground train station by the bald bricklayers by the oyster-selling seafood vendors by the preaching screeching Bible boombox Nigerian by the parksleeping and been-here-six-months-and-they-say-no-jobs-my-friend eastern Europeans by the pigeon-strewn church are all

green.

~

It starts off in the decaying glory of Hackney Wick. The wickerman burns. On the terraces overlooking the manic cranes of the Olympic games there's some serious barbecue mania. Then the performance art bands. Then the self-styled artists vomiting on each other. Then the warehouse parties with 1980s New York nostalgia.

On the bridge by the highway to Victoria Park, lovers reunite, licking each other, hemmed in by the white noise of cars. Next to them, someone's painted a scroll sign: 'Go on, jump!' I see it all, a cyclops eye burned into my forehead.

Then scram. Back to the old haunts on Brick Lane. We start off in 1001 cafe for the Scheherazade nights. Stories eating into each other. Endless oceans. Speed-kids and Rastas flyer outside. Armenian bouncers scare with their *Matrix* get-ups. Sunlight bulbs melt on large wooden tables and chairs where the hipsters incorporated (glitter lipstick) and the homeless (sores of eyes) and the beggars (deepvoiced and canister-shaking) and the junkies (black teeth and cumstained jumpers) and the cabbies (always Bangladeshi) fuse and fizzle. I need my fix.

I scope the nightstreets, looking for Shah-Jehan. That's the dealer's name. Bangladeshi kid with Mughal dreams. Baseball cap, a stubble goatee, gold chain dangling. He's been in and out of jail over the past year. He invests in gold saving up for his sister's wedding. First time I met him, he asked me to guess how old he was. Him and a Somali mate of his. I did. Correctly (twenty-one, nineteen). *You gonna make somethin of your life, brov!* he said, eyeing me with the moon of his eyes.

I wait at the corner of Brick Lane and Heneage Street. Shah-Jehan emerges from the shadows, bulldog on chain. He's not alone. Behind him are his brothers, sickle & chain. *Gimme a minute brov, usual yeah? Charlie, pills, skunk, yeah?* They're now running on Brick Lane. Another Bangladeshi boy is seen, skinning a samosa. One of Shah-Jehan's friends — long-haired and spotted nose — grabs him by the shirt, rams him up against a car. The other kids force the car door open. Place the boy's head in the vacuum. Slam the car door shut. Blood bursts. I stand opposite, motionless. Shah-Jehan waves to me, places his forefinger on his lips. *Shhhhh...*

Ten minutes later, he walks up to me, hands me my stuff. He gives me credit. I walk over to 1001. Head to the stained toilet, slip out my powder with a wipe of the seat. Outside I hear the long drizzle of yellow. I search frantically for an old used telephone card. Find it, then fold a fiver. Chop chop, line up. *Sniiiiiiiiiiiiiiiiiiffffffffffffffff*. Chalk crack, baby laxative, coca-cola burn my nosehairs. Do it again. And again. Save a smidgen of the half-gram for later. Slipslide outside.

Head to the inner temple which is pumping red. It's close to midnight. I see the usual faces, all ages. Near the bar a scuffle breaks out over weed. It's drum & bass crazy and the place sweats like tropical skin. An hour passes, and I feel it's time. I pull out a superman-sign starshaped pill with pink edges. Pop goes the weasel. Now I play the waiting game, the whites of my eyes getting beadier all the time. I check out the girls. Animal intention. Tinfoil fairy wings. Bubbles of wonder.

There's an old woman by the stage, etched face, the blitz on her face, burning with joy. Next to her, a dreaded girl checks herself out in the mirror, watched on by two Turks in red shirts. It's getting immense and bright like a supernova. Explosion is as explosion does. I need to split.

I head out on the streets, and the warm glow of the sun-bulbed streetlights nourishes me. I'm walking on the moon. I walk past the pollution-fighting-banadana-wearing new-world-order graffiti-staring onto the paperbag streets, signalling my way through to the church of Spitalfields (and the Spitz has been torn down, and the ten bells is quiet, and the old underground pisser that's been converted to a club is starting to shake and drum and thrum and throb) to the cold night air of glorious Londontown.

I walk down Commercial Street, which looks slight like the scaggy
corners of SoHo and Tribeca in New York, bastard brother staking
his claim.

~

The old buildings with scabbed windows are green dinosaurs.
Posters advertising every kind of imaginable after-party hang
like old green canvases. The Lebanese cafe that stealths as a
hash hangout is still open. Green. I cross over to 54
(studio? I don't know. It don't say). I knock on a big green door.

A minute later, it's open sesame and I enter to full-frontal
face a bearded African bouncer. Green. He lets me in.
The upper level of the bar is eerily quiet, the lights toned down,
green. But wait, hush hush, I hear dark-bass-sounds rollicking.
I take the steps down and oh oh oh my here we go,
the pump hits my head hard.

On the dance floor, it's a secret ritual —

fluorescent green sticks, naked legs and tight jeans,
emerald glasses, and the coming-to-and-fro of hot green bodies.
Everyone's in love. Sucking skin, tribality.
I see people dance in their green heads, their bodies becoming
the ideas of their minds, elastic, green.

Electricity fudges the mind.

I start seeing in
holograms and jump cuts and flash forwards and jump cuts and
flash forwards and jump cuts and flash forwards and
jump cuts and

flash!

I'm on my own. I step outside, greeted by the superman green of a magic London sky.

New age prophet. Blinded by sunlight.

Indigo, Bandra

I sweat an old Goan woman's dress by the delta of Chapel Road —

Bandra, Bombay.

Paper skin, pockmarked pink skirt, her top the indigo green of the sea her Portuguese piedog voyagers ploughed through to set up shop in these islands four centuries ago.

I smell her coconut hair, the bombil fish of her laugh.

I morph into the woodskin of her carved walking stick.

Her oil slips into my mouth, sandman in eye, and I as a walking stick which bears her hunchback, the hump of her breasts, I see

woodshavings spewed in dust, dengue-fevered garbage-fires burning like Iraqi oil fields on the open road, the

stun of art-deco edging Bandra bandstand, the old Chinese joint called Jimmy's Kitchen with American chopsuey to clog your arteries, and there all around

in installation caves, Bandra's comic graffiti — zebras fucking on old shuttered doors, reclining Shiva-faces, monkey gods with bells in their ears.

Round red-lingam chillies crackling like static in late afternoon sun, an old fisherwoman spreads and lofts saris that hang in the air like mosquitoes, like incipient rain, and then crack and fall like parachutes.

I see lime-juice sellers and Tamil women — intestines of white flowers in their bunned hair — selling statues of gods and men.

And there rushing towards me — a woman with a stick, a dog in heat by the garbagemound, incense in wood-nose —

a Goan black Christ in the arms of a Mary, God-whore, carnival-stilted, carnival sounded with sea-guitars & trumpets, crosses born by hard brown skin as the indigo lights of early evening flare like Roman candles and the songs of prayer

hallelujah the road to life. Toxic megacity waltz.

Christ comes to me, eats my woodflesh with his tobacco-stained teeth, sucks the dry pistachio o' my breasts, and sticks me like a dildo in the caves of his throat.

There I hear the hymns o' Bandra, the activated electronica of its clubs, moshed with tabla rhythms. Bandra now.

The Portuguese are gone but their churches are still here, with our singing voices stretched taut and joyous across the young

measled skin of the Bombay sky.

Doctor Sahib

I have taken my oath
and witnessed
many a great scene —

stomachs concave in time,
legs in crawl like spiders,
wailing Medusas,
arched backs
bursting,

heads hung like convicts —
faces of eyes.

There have also been
limbs floating weightless

in space,

cartilage fly-fed,
brains in mud,

sounds mangled,
breath speared.

I have sewn together
bags of bones, and under a

microscope, studying the
cells of centuries and the
plasma of ambition, have
seen the battle for natural selection.

Let me tell you, my boy —

If you wage wars against
Turks and Romans, or the vast
armies of Napoleon,

remember always to
eat bread soaked in the
fat of a sacrificed animal —

woollen clothes and a hat
insure consistent circulation of blood.

Proverbs

I

I hitch a ride to Glasgow for no reason. I check into a dingy shared hostel-room where I meet a wanderer from Iceland. He tells me stories about whaling in cold waters. His hands are veined and strong. He's just got a divorce. He came to Glasgow with a friend who stole his dough. He works as a security guard sometimes. He's out of cash but he knows the city's secrets. Its dives of damnation.

We go out drinking that night. Glasgow's rough and ready. I don't remember much save for hustling our way into a private gig at a bar. There's music inside and the band's playing some wicked American funk. They're white and peachily Scottish and they call themselves The Confederation of the Disco Pimps. I laugh and smoke cheap drum. The Icelander plays wet behind the ears. I'm a gullible fool and I pay for his drinks. We head back to the hostel, eating cheap Chinese take-away. The next morning, I wake up to find the whaler gone. With my duffel bag. I walk the streets of the old town and I find a little cafe with little old ladies who look at me like I'm a strange alien. I take out my dogeared notebook and start to write.

II

The alien writes poems about a poet who loved Blake and took his proverbs from hell a bit too seriously. *The road of excess leads to the palace of wisdom* was his favourite. And so the poet spent his years making this his mantra.

He starts smoking dope as a kid, hitchhikes through the known galaxy like a beaten soul. He discovers Rimbaud and Genet and Burroughs, slits his veins with dynamite street jazz, lacquers his eyes with Greek mythology. He cultivates androgyny as a polemical gesture. He takes what he can get, sleeps with whatever's open. In the midst of hard living, he forgets to write. There are little rat-curved lines, a few aphorisms like *when in doubt fuck a cat with horns* but there's little of substance. And so one day, he decomposes.

III

The black coffee in front of me — black as the devil, as hot as hell, as sweet as a girl, so said a teacher once — is cold. The little old ladies are gone. It's time to go home.

IV

I hitchhike my way back to the Big Smoke, which is pretty smoky. I spend the days sleeping or looking at clouds. And smoking reefer. Some sticky stuff called 'lemon'. From the streets of Mile End from a chap called The Candyman. He sells me stuff in bags with batman signs and naked girls. I go back to my tiny cold room which has no heat, get inspired by the sound of that great London creature — the mouse — and I continue writing.

V

I start dreaming eerie London dreams. I see whales floating over Whitechapel. Dolphin dopamine. I see a little girl open the palm of her hands to reveal a floating diamond and a dead crow being eaten by tiny red ants. I dream of a man on a beach, a great moon-mountain Union Jack planted behind him. Through the cut of a camera shot, we see a family slitted through house-fences. The sun — *busy olde foole* — is out in force. As they smile, beaming towards my fish-eye lens, we hear a voice over that could be the thunder of a pagan god — 'and who did we build this England for...' it asks over and over and over and over again. The silent movie melts slowly to a heap of skulls. Fade away. Reappear.

VI

Next morning, when I awake I feel I have grown as big as a dinosaur, as sly as a robot. I hover over the canal by the bridge. I remember something that Borges once said but the exact words slip away, slip away, slip away...

Coming soon to this location...
BEAUTIFUL RUINS

Cybosaurus

It is with cities as it is with sex. We seek the physical city and find only a conglomeration of private cells. In the city as nowhere else we are reminded that we are individuals, units. Yet the idea of the city remains; it is the god of the city that we pursue, in vain.
V. S. Naipaul, The Mimic Men

I

I tell my android wife I use simple words. Now on, keeping things simple is the complex thing. No taut reference to gods (dead), cities (carved), death (bones), history (becoming), poetry (porn), nothing.

And most of all any twaddle on art or form will tell me I'm dead. I have nothing to give, to wretch. When I feel greasy & clogged — rivers of arteries — I'll inspire myself by munching chicken bones. Crunch.

Or if I'm eloquent it'll be aubergine pasta — dark indigo-skinned, brie-melt, cut-roast black pepper cannibals — with a sprinkle of rocket salad. Clover, cardamom, the drill. Simple.

II

In February, oceans later, the city becomes a

cracked gin-glass of

drizzle.

III

Four & fifty years have I lived here, not born here. City of cadaver exiles. Rimbaud, Marx, Gandhi, Hendrix. Productive darkness.

I hide my mutant amoebae. My dog-eat dustbins. My space-haloes. My frog-antennas. My cyber-switches. My strategies against architecture. My face is Munch.

Tears can't stream from balloon faces, puffed apparitions, gay lord fictions, this city I've seen is full of whores & fairies, spittle & damask, dreams soaked in black ale.

In winter, when there is no sky — 'gunmetal sky', 'fish-scale sky', 'cast-iron sky' you get my drift? — yes when there is no sky

>(start, stop,

>>start again)

the train that rumbles over Cambridge Heath when a black-midget beer-guzzling beggar shoots his mind with porno dreams & the scrivener canvasses with drum & bass, the hollow dubstep cave of the echo-train brain

>bombs my finger to silence.

IV

I'm old, I'm old, I'll wear my condoms Rizla-rolled. Rain wrecks my libido. I speak coming from far Turkish(tonic) lands where saintly citadels(skywalking), raisined rice(startrecked), mint tea(flying robots), and the hot beating heart of the Mediterranean(Andromeda) sun makes me stand in salutation.

(whose voice do I speak in? Who is this

                      ghost in the machine?)

Here I love smut. Smut and more smut — jagged stiletto smiles, iced vodka, rain-slick lipstick in a dank Soho street. Pornshop elastica. Red-ribboned curtains.

Arab businessman. Cockney-speaking, beard-wearing Muslim bouncers. Russian poletap strippers. The spiced jiggle o' flesh.

                Should I go on?

V

Surely I must have music left in me.
    (Note-ghosts lift from sky-vapours)

        Simulated life, tweet-wrecker incarnate. The city
                                      is a
  spider-

     -webbed-

        -market.

Everything is unreal, staged, lied upon. I am the apothecary of simulacra. I sell phantom emotions.

Inside my blood beats — like sub-bass electro — in isolated spasms.

    This is the great
                      Theatre of the Awkward.

VI

The city chooses through whom it speaks. Hollow arteries, emotion suggestion, flaccid temper.

Once it's chosen the atom-human-cyborg machine (call it Cybosaurus?) the city must drain-pipe, throat-sliver him-her-it.

(what am I saying?

Speak without consequence.
Speak immediacy. Speak rhythm.
Speak in skulls. Speak dope. Speak easy.
Speak unruly. Speak in scales. Speak mutant disco.

Speak Chewbacca. Speak tornado. Speak conquistador.
Speak simulacra. Speak in fish dialect.
Speak Isadora, Q-lab, Dalston dirty condom-

                                                    (-inium)

Speak
       rat-a-
              tat-tat-tat...

speak Angola. Speak fishnet stockings.
Speak zumba. Speak protons. Speak androids.
Speak cyber-graffiti.
Speak haemorrhoids.

Speak string theory. Speak antinomies. Speak plato's retreat.
Speak anglo-saxon, Michael Jackson, tooty-frooty
                                        fornication.

Speak cellular Andromeda.
Speak black-hole flash fiction.

Speak auto-autopsy psychobabble-
fish.

Speak in
neutrinos, in marmalade, in hot-flavour sado-masoch-
ism,

speak grizzlybear.

VII

The Cybosaurus is a soulless animal. Transformer-human. Egg-shell head, antennae wings of arms.

Tongue is brain is satellite mapping.

Love for it is a tweet-deck. Mirrors of our corporate clones. Clones of our bone-prophets. Domes of central church — St Paul's spiralling into ether like hairs of a galaxy. Like apocalypse,

(in fashion)

The plunger reaches heaven, is a weather system crash. Shards of the brown river incubate. Rats ruffle.

(The city is a mirage.
                An ellipse...)

VIII

Street-people — low-life high-tech beggars & bankers — have dog-sniffed your cybosaurus soul. They hunt in wolf-packs. Their faces are blank but ominous like the weather. Threat of rain. Fuck off menace. Your violent thoughts suck violence centripedally. The way you form words in your mind has changed. Everything is television. Static cereal. Caramelised philosophy. Onions of guilt. Form wounds.

>(window wisdom:
>   clouds passing)

IX

None of this is the city. All of it is you.
        Thinking is action.
How did you grow so old? Even a cybosaurus sheds tears on skin like paper.
Your walking stick is a memory chip. Ship of fools.
(that's all the magic you're given)

At night, you come back home walking across ancient silent Roman streets littered with plastic, syringes, blood. Old tooth decay.

You clock down, tube-down oesophagus alley stained, rivered with piss in which you see your iPad eyes. Piss-plasma reflects ghosts of the last battle.

Outside aluminium doors, as you fumble for a key-pad soaked in Prometheus silt, shaped in glass mirages, a crackwhore dinosaur offers you her gestation services. You radioactivate, melt to ash in starlight. Slip like a lizard to your bunk bed.

Ash forms human turd. You sit on the edge of your bed, coolie-squatting. A couple cries in fuck-motions above you.

Your cyborg eyes make mirrors splinter.

Bad luck in dreams.

X

Tell your dreams to bleed.

Scratch.

Beer bottles.

Tunnels of darkness.

Hemmed in by mirrors.

The sun like Einstein.

Float-limbed, ivory bearded — a father flying above Iberian waters. Gold hair with his baby son.

Icaurus,
      Dedalus,
           diphtheria.

Blue is
      the colour
           of
                this dream
                        falling...

XI

    ... into flash-mobs of cavernous light.

Caucasians everywhere.
    Plato's cave meshed with bees. Everywhere.

    Bees hang off beards. Bees slip on tongues.
    Bees shelter in ear-caves. Bees butterfly.
    Bees form cosmos. Bees___zzz. Be....... es.

    Cogito ergo Fukushima.

    Three Caucasians like Simon, Olivia and Paul drink
    coffee made of bees.

'Where's this coffee made? Africa?'

XII

And more. Wake up as a child in a pillow-paper, yellow-walled room. Thick single mattress, books everywhere. Dark but white light in the kitchen outside. You lift and hear your father's dead voice and radio static. Old woman-bead-lovers. Rosary red. You lift again like inverted parachutes. You are young & old. Sudden, your father's brown hand wrenches through a fold of skin. He pulls out your liver. Your liver in his hand is a bleeding radio.

XIII

Cybosaurus comes across Aborigines. Feels kinship.
His colour is alien-green.

He sees star-dots, brain-waves. Bright seeming colours.
Rainbow serpents. Eating, swallowing people. Shitting them into yellow dream-clots. Becoming circles in the desert landscape.

Rainbow serpent, I-robot, snake of guns.
Red snake-fire. Electric blue birds.

(He wonders why ancient cultures imagined serpents as magic matter-coils, roots of the universe)

>When fire dreams it folds into geometry.

>>Isosceles triangles.

>Trigonometaphors.   Jagged right-angles.

>>Totem stick-figures
>>with
>>algorithmic souls.

(Aboriginal imagination, rock carvings, dance of water hold all our Sci-Fi memories.
>Open sesame...)

A python is a boomerang. It always comes back.
Mandalas, mulga trees, salt plains, stony country. Imagery of sand.
The Tube is a rattlesnake.

Wild turkey dreams of amoeba.
Honey ant dreams of syphilis circles speared with train tracks.
Child dreams of sepia tattoos.
Two women dream of rectangles.
Bandicoot dreams of strands of sun-hair.
Old man dreams of canoes, rivers, starships.
Worm dreams of ice cubicles, alien algebra
                                        (xxyz***~mc~)
Skeleton dreams of a mop & whiskey.
Flying cockroach dreams of chicken wings.
Rain dreams of iguana.
Stars dream of natty dreadlocks.
Possum dreams of granite shapes.
Snake dreams of punk Mohawks.
Water dreams of milky way, galactica.
Seed dreams of ant dreaming a wave dreaming a hole in mouth of a
                                              dreaming black-
                        hole...
Morning star, sand-fly, sacred kimonos.
                                    Star-sweat.

(Wandjina figures in ancient Australia by the river are

        Lucas aliens.
        Epilogue is prologue.
                A mosquito is a cyclone.)

Mediterranean

    I

She lifts ships with
seadrip in her eyelash —

foam grows in hairshades, her forearm
brinks like a precipice.

In eye, she gave me her
crinkle of hair, clothed in
aubergines.

Cooked me, fed me horsemeat.

I grew to a cyclops. I fashioned my
world-drift, logging dreams, one by one,
jutting them like fishing nets in Mediterranean.

The fog lifts. She waves me away
in granita sip. Facing, we spoke the
art of war in a square by a bookstore, fitted in gargoyles,
ambling.

I lived through scars in my teeth.
I storied her, foiling the
stab of whiskey, vomitfresh in a bar basin,

somewhere in Chicago.

    II

I give her my lizard skin, plumed. My
ashtray of a laugh, stunned.
I slip beneath her footsteps. Coil.

She will sail, anchorfresh,
cigarette-smoked, free.

My heart is a sock, machine-washed.

My skull splits in the colour of three dreams —
redcoated, seadeep, scarecrowed.

Black electricity wires my lung. Burns

eye, alone,

still.

The Muckworm

Two warheads from Chechnya mushrooming in my hands. American eyes bartered in gold coins. Baghdad's looted treasures in the spilt foam of my pocket.

My head's decked with Shanghai pearls, snakeskin jackets in Hong Kong, where ming-lords served me the keys to their kingdom husked in the liver of a dragon.

I cruiselined my way to the Himalayas, cutting the ocean to craters. Pashmina shawls, dogturd hash I smoked with the Taliban. They'd green crystals dangled like demonic suns from their beards, black tar opium, dreamsunked like stockmarket crash. I gave no one no change.

I'd caucasian bellydancers licking the welt of my heels. I vamped up sausage palaces in Berlin, bleeding east to west. There's a checkpoint scar on my chest with chamber knives, panopticon whispers.

I waded through nuclear nights in London, where a fat man eating the innards of a boar, drinking sewage from the city's secret rivers, taught me the pleasures of blue rain, frog's wine. I stole his parked throat, his voice in my gauche jacket, sniped the nerve-endings of his bilious ancestry.

I became the master of voices. Rats crawled in my tongue incubating forked languages. My face morphed to a map, chock-a-blocked with cityscape infinites. I heard dreams, my neutrons charged with new world jazz.

I hedgefunded my path to El Dorado, whipped up desert-storm cocktails in Manhattan, ate Rockerfeller's ghost for breakfast, puking the yoke of his ire — I did it all, cigared like Castro, neoneyed.

O ye toads, grovelling in the ooze of your poverty, I slaved once on the intestine streets of a botched city by the Arabian sea, carrying the weight of blackdevil cows on my back, gunrunning for sailors, empire builders, underworld actors.

Alleyed in slumslime, edged by a skyscraper of white marble, a sheikh from the desert stuck a gun to my temple, its heat singeing my skin. He coughed, the tongue of his beard in my ear, 'Recite, heathen! and I'll give you my oil as worship.' I plunged in the holy fire-histories of my era.

Now, I pile up bones, govern the world, suck out the eyes of the poor. My empire is nuclear potential, my wealth a telepathic spider, webbing global dreams in proton chips. I give no one no change. I sleep the dreams of lepers, huddled, alone.

The Living and the Dead

I left home. Belly hungry. Scorched sun, parched earth.
Babies like foetuses. Clan wars, tribal wars. Sister raped,
brothers bombed. Carcasses watched and
eaten by vultures. God's forgotten people.

I left with the devil in my heart. Met a man with a beard and
turban who promised me paradise. Crossed desert and
mountain and sea. On a boat, tattered and flimsy.
The curse of the sun. Rats eating my flesh.

I felt I was the Messiah.

After a hundred days and a hundred nights,
I landed near the promised land. Planes dropped bombs.
Others were detained in camps, packed like cattle.
In the distance, on a boat docked, I heard the
turbaned voices of my brothers
stretching across the ocean and sky.

'No country of our own,' they sang, sand in their throats.
How do we go on? We travel the world, we're promised shelter.
We die trying, but even the shadowy cries of our corpses
don't move these uniforms and guns. No, we're starved
even more till our eyes fall out. Our eyes fall
on cold prison slaughterhouse floors. And then and then and
then... when we die, our ghosts crawl out like worms from the

cold dead, cracking skin of our bodies, our ghosts slipping out like
sweat, and our ghosts grow muscle tissue bones hair blood, and

then they finally see us. Sipping raki and smoking cheroots,
they say 'okay okay we take you in, we give you shelter
from the storm'. Our ghosts are more alive than when we were
living, and laughing, our ghosts leap into the promised land
with milk in our eyes. And then we, dark

bands of brothers, stumble and fall
on hard cobbled streets, dainty avenues
lined with pink limestone churches
carved out of shadows of mosques and the
stinging pasta sounds of white laughter and
champagne and
the clink of expensive knives and forks, and the
sticky cheese which smells like rotting
flesh they eat
and the curse of wealth that we
dream into distant stars
invades our cotton-thin ghostly skins
like armies of tanks and we
hate ourselves even more in death.

We look for jobs that ghosts do,
picking oranges and tomatoes, sifting through rubbish.
Even their dogs scare us.
As ghosts we are seen only when they choose to see.
And then we are chased from cities and picture-postcard

towns and villages where masked men carrying guns,
swastikas in mouths, promising Golden Dawns,
force us to hide in forest and bush, carving and
sculpting huts out of cardboard and plastic.

When it rains we move.
Country to country, begging.
We make music with our bones.

And then one day, our own brothers betray
us and we are found late at night by
booted warriors, defenders of the faith, and they
kill us again, stab us again, and it is only when they
do that they know that we were already
dead, that the blood of a ghost cannot be seen or smelt.

Only when the sunlight slinks through the trees next morning,
and the world of this paradise is silent, and the spirits of our
gods rise across oceans, does this blood, our warm holy blood,
split into the colours of a nova, a rainbow in the sky.

Once Upon a Time in New York

NYC, monochrome. The crack of poolballs. Noise of breakdancers on the sidewalk. Flashing neon. Goldtoothed smiles of dopedealers in Washington Square Park. Gyro meat, Macdougal street. Subway sirens. Hot dog & roasted-nut smells wafting through the air. C'mon — one dollar, only one dollar! Manhattan attitude. Fuck you man, find it yourself! Long-haired Latino women who look you up & down. Hare Krishnas selling copies of the Gita in St. Marks Place. Sexed up smiles from strangers you never see again. Traffic scenes on 6th ave, with peeps hanging outta their cars, yelling at god. Midnight pickups. Silent on Bleeker street. Stars like dew. Lampglow on Houston. Absolute vodka billboards. Bile seeping through liver-city. Winstons. Nicotine warmth. Maybe someone on Prince. Yawning, tummy-scratching graffiti artists. Bandicoots. Drunk preachers. A shout on the street. God is watching and

I'm drinking in a bar in New York — I don't remember anyone else being there with me. At some point, I finish my drink, get out of the bar, and this guy who was sitting next to me, follows me out. I'm here in Manhattan, at the corner of West 4th and Broadway, and I'm strutting on Broadway like I used to, and this guy from the bar runs up behind me and takes out a gun. I vaguely hear him, he's across the street now and he takes aim and I try to run and avoid his archery, scared as shit, and he shoots twice and I can't see and both times he gets me hard in the stomach a little to the left and I don't feel no pain but I watch myself in slowmotion fall faintly and slow & easy die with a thud.

Moments later, I'm walking the streets again. Down Lafayette, but I have a strange feeling of 'being' dead. I am a ghost. Good ole Hamlet. I keep walking and walking and at another corner I look into the glass window of this shop with the news on the TV screen and I see myself dead, being talked about. Images of police cars, ambulances, sirens like whirling dervishes.

Don't know how the dream ends (can a dream ever end or begin?) but now I'm in this old dilapidated house. A friend's place, in a real dump. It's not NYC anymore but probably some old rat-infested alley in North Calcutta. I'm in a small apartment. A tiny congested flat with green-shuttered windows, rusty grills, broken tiles, insect ivy, saris hung and stretched like shrouds. And I talk with these people I have never met in my life. These friends of mine & I converse, smoke heavy black-hash spliffs, laugh like hyenas. But I'm not happy. And in my dream I wake up and I'm back in New York as I hear sirens scream past my window. Doppler effect. Blood pulsates through every nerve, every fibre of the city. I strain to catch the shape of these cop-cars but I'm greeted instead by the red glow of lights tingling far away like hot flame tongues. I remember the shock of those sirens. And I remember turning away from the window and looking 'round the apartment and I see empty deformed cigarette packs, a half empty packet of chips, dirty underwear and socks littered on the bed, piles of clothes like garbage dumps, a bottle of Jack glinting in yellow lamplight and I remember wondering what my mother would've thought of all this. And slowly my stoned gaze falls on the TV screen pulsating with silent images. Somewhere in California a Latino shopowner had been murdered by young white men. The deceased's face, moving on the screen like an amorphous globule of spit, flashed and flashed. I reach for the remote in a cold panic, numb, indifferent and confused. I change the channel and see a snake slithering along the underbelly of a dense forest, Madonna moving in black and white, shows on social anxiety disorders, country music, football mania, buy two get one free, what would you do if your wife fucked other men, behind the music on Motley Crew and I hit the volume control, 'We were so screwed up, we were injecting alcohol in our veins, that's when I said to myself — dude, this is f***ed up' I mean what was wrong with us, we could't just drink alcohol we had to inject it!' And I remember switching off the TV or maybe I became a rock god like Jimmy Page and just pushed it out off the window onto some poor passerby but I turned away and towards a sheet of paper in front of me, illuminated by the table lamp, and I stared blankly out into the artificial New York sky and I wrote down these words, spelt clearly in a dream:

I want to go home, I want to go home, I want to go home!

Digital Monsoon

Car, white Ambassador,   enters New Market,
    Calcutta.   Woman gets out with
girl of ten, boy of five.

Sweating like meat, they smile.

Mother gets out with   girl of ten,
    boy of five.   Father's head stays
in,   cooked in summer heat. Herd of

moustachioed men   yell to help park car,
    cumbersome. Mosquitoes hover like
vultures in   puddles of rain.

Girl holds mother's   hand, boy
    skips round.   Car jerks forward
back, father   lifts eyebrow at
        potbellied policeman,

casually squashing his male child.
Voices swell like bellies.

Wife opens mouth,   does not
    scream. Men,   tongues wriggling,

on seeing the dead,   its head a

    spade with little hairs, and
not knowing,   sma-
ash
    carwindows.

Cop who saw crime,   stops tamasha,
    makes order. Crowd falls
silent.   Father's head hits
                      steering wheel.

Saris, wraps of   festering fruit,
    Float wide free of web,
Sweat of fume,   in summer

Hovered over   by impending monsoon.
    Milk-heavy.
Fade to black.

Hackney Fragments

— A white Jamaican, brov!

— You seen an American in a kilt?

— Don't know if I wanna see that. Men's dresses. Them don't float my boat.

— I told 'im to gimme a wet smoochy big slob of a kiss!

— Tellin ya baby, yes you're a pain in the arse!

~

This is my London day these winters. Cold rain, summer far away. Fly on the wall. Coffee mind. Mind mind why do I spend so much time in my head mind mind? Little that happens on these rainswept streets pulls me out of mind. Mind. Taking 26 or 388, from four to six, through Hackney road from Shoreditch cauldron empty houses bricklayed houses little chimneys little sidestreets shut shop shutters puerile 'east is the new west' signs what happens in mind steel trains on rock tunnels council estate vulture shine endless fried chicken shop shine kensey fried dixie fried perfect fried Brooklyn fried almost fried eastwest fried Alabama fried Mississippi fried Dallas fried Charlie Parker fried chickchickchickchickchicken yes yes yes storefront black barbershop stripclub leaning pole gleaming cockney scheming buzzzzzz canal pretty houses oh so pretty houses warehouses arty farty houses and then that beautiful truly lovely madly beautiful gaswork dinosaur gaswork by Haggerston by Broadway market and then 'Mare street Well street' on the bus voiceover and then through endlessly ethnic Hackney central then when it happens —

> Two vested blackskinshimmering boxers sparring in front of Hackney town hall
> Watched on spied on shopped on eagerly white bloke blooming a pink umbrella

— there is a grim beauty that swathes east London in chromatic light

~

Someone scribbled this onto the rock crust of bus-seat:

> 'listen to this. Fuck sake the fucking train came straight away so we didn't have time to swap cigarettes and I didn't give his oyster card back, what a piss take, and he's going on holiday for three weeks on Monday. God in hell! Lucky I love him innit love!?'

~

Two Jamaican men on a bus by Trelawney estate:

— I was calling ya!

— I didn't hear ya!

— I was calling ya!

— I went to da funeral...dem say da sun shine ya know?!

~

St Mary of Eton Church. Bus stop. West African man, with lilt of Hackney on his lips, approaches me with a card for a Christian conversion. He starts his bible beat. He ain't blastin like a boombox. He speaks with certain gestures, eyes contractable — 'there's nothing wrong cheerin for Chelsea, being in a pub. You go through experiences, good and bad, mostly bad, and then you become the truth. There's a reality. No wrong thoughts, no wrong convictions, no wrong deeds. Coz the reality is the cemetery. Grave after grave. Talented people. So you gotta know the truth. There's nothing wrong.' And then he smiles, teeth glaring. I shake his bearing, slipslide into bus. Climb steps. Seat in a window. Watch the spurs of hair glisten like glass on his head.

~

This is knife capital. Everyday in the local papers, kids killing getting killed. Yesterday someone said there's a bloke who heads into a pisser in London fields, afternoon, sunshining lido swimming, people playing sunlit beauty. He steps in at the wrong time. A guy with a mask stabs him for the fun of it.

~

Nightime endless parties. Hackney wick dalston empowering church passing clouds all of it slipslide makeup man hipsters too cool too cool and the best music in the world surely this must be — funky funk Latin Cuban Balkan Turkish Indian drumnbass jazz top that shit! This the real deal. Inside warehouses, electronica rages like a tornado, people gear up n shake, a Nigerian Belarusian demonwoman growls through conch shells make foxwolf noises like foxes at night in Clapton foxing like baby strangles raping, she sings she sings a bass guitar back vocal sampler shaking doubling tripling her voice fox becomes loaded leaded in hackney wick canal backing empty nightmagenta sky she sings she growls she makes animals incubation tribal trancelike spiritual shaminations I hear the shake of ancient forests in her voice amen omen we sail into nightships unaware...

Ricorso

I

This dream — like others — is not fantastical in the least. I've always been jealous of girlfriends who'd see grotesque half-human half-animal species, fire-mountains, men with heads made of octopus arms. No, mine are strangely placid, prosaic, even dull in their resemblance to everyday reality. Which makes them all the more confusing. Perhaps.

What I remember now is that I'm in New York, but it looks like it could be the edge of Kemps Corner in Bombay. Or the corner of East Houston. Perhaps I'm in a strange amalgamation of these two cities. (Am I condemned forever to write of the same old places, over and over again?) But what I recall are sensations, images of a great studded brown skyscraper, and the amphibian sounds of a city as it wakes to frenetic life in rush-hour mornings. And we glide — I'm sure there are others with me, pied pipers of urban mythologies — we glide down avenues bearing strange tales of death and decay, and these avenues now narrow imperceptibly to a glimmering post-industrial wasteland in Hackney Wick. And the colours remain — pastels and oils. Mucus tones.

And we now turn a corner and find ourselves in a vast underground carpark, a cramped artistic aerodrome. There are people inside, seated on chairs, steel and aluminium, and in front of them, a male speaker, hipster guru with a striped maroon mackintosh, gesticulating with ivory arms. Behind him in an elongated power-point frame, a dark screen in which fish-fleets come and go. A screen of fish in indigo waters. The hipster lectures confidently, the screen is his backdrop, bloated.

In a whirlwind, the frames switch, and in a state of lucid dreaming I witness and scribe through sensations of urban dereliction, beautiful mahoganies. Patinas, fragments, chopped freeze-frames promising renewal. Thatched carvings, brick-layers, spittle.

And then I'm back in the television room in Calcutta, and I'm seated on the armchair reserved for my dead father and now on the bed opposite, seated on bedsheets covered in blue fish, where I'd sit to watch cricket, is Amit Chaudhuri, the novelist. I kid you not. And I see his well-brought-up fringe of greying hair, and the comic spectacles, and a stitched woollen jumper for Calcutta winters. And he's speaks to me in the voice of his book on the city, he speaks of modernity, of urban ruins, the noise and fury of city-addiction.

He continues speaking to me like an oracle of ancient mysteries, and then I find myself headed to teach bored students in Mile End and as the train approaches on a cold winter morning in the Wick, the chipped slit of daylight beneath the train tracks gives me a glimpse of a parking lot, graffiti-strewn, and a single burning can of fire in the snow, and a man, an old weary prophet of the ages. He wanders from burnt firewood to dismantled parts of broken cars and then back to abandoned trailer-trash, and I see him collect wood, the cold and snow are mere shadows, and he picks and collects, picks and collects, walks to the burning bush of his prophecy and feeds the fire, which spits and crackles, spits and crackles, speaking in impeccable nuance.

Train passes, I hop on.